Henry Purcell

KEYBOARD WORKS

Edited by

William Barclay Squire

Dover Publications, Inc., New York

Published in Canada by General Publishing Company, Ltd.,
30 Lesmill Road, Don Mills, Toronto, Ontario.
Published in the United Kingdom by Constable and Company,
Ltd.

This Dover edition, first published in 1990, is a republication
of *Suites, Lessons and Pieces for the Harpsichord (Original
Works for the Harpsichord)*, edited by William Barclay Squire
and originally published in four volumes by J. & W. Chester,
London and Brighton, in 1918. The French version of the Preface
has been omitted, and a table of contents and a publisher's note
have been added. We are grateful to the Music Library of Indiana
University for lending a portion of the music for reproduction.

Manufactured in the United States of America
Dover Publications, Inc., 31 East 2nd Street, Mineola, N.Y.
11501

Library of Congress Cataloging-in-Publication Data

Purcell, Henry, 1659–1695.
  [Harpsichord music]
  Keyboard works.

  Reprint. Originally published: Suites, lessons, and pieces.
London : J. & W. Chester, 1918.
  1. Harpsichord music.   I. Squire, William Barclay, 1855–1927.
I. Title.
M22.P98S7   1990   90-751444
ISBN 0-486-26363-0

CONTENTS

Suite in G Major, Z. 660 — 1
Prelude, 1. Almand, 2. Corant, 2. Minuet, 3.

Suite in G Minor, Z. 661 — 4
Prelude, 4. Almand, 6. Corant, 8. Saraband, 9.

Suite in G Major, Z. 662 — 10
Prelude, 10. Almand, 12. Corant, 14.

Suite in A Minor, Z. 663 — 16
Prelude, 16. Almand, 16. Corant, 18. Saraband, 19.

Suite in C Major, Z. 666 — 20
Prelude, 20. Almand, 22. Corant, 23. Saraband, 23.

Suite in D Major, Z. 667 — 24
Prelude, 24. Almand, 25. Hornpipe, 27.

Suite in D Minor, Z. 668 — 28
Prelude, 28. Corant, 30. Hornpipe, 31.

Suite in F Major, Z. 669 — 32
Prelude, 32. Almand, 33. Corant, 34. Minuet, 36.

Trumpet Tune, called the Cibell, Z. T678 — 37

Trumpet Tune in C Major, Z. T697 — 38

A Ground in Gamut, Z. 645 — 39

Almand in C Major, from Suite, Z. 665 — 41

Saraband with Division, Z. 654 — 42

Voluntary in C Major, Z. 717 — 43

A Verse in F Major, Z. 716 — 44

Trumpet Tune in D Major — 45

Air in D Minor, Z. T675 — 46

Air in D Minor, Z. T676 — 47

Ground in C Minor, Z. T681 — 48

Prelude in A Minor, Z. 652 — 50

Toccata in A Major, Z. D229 — 52

Hornpipe in E Minor, Z. T685 — 62

Air in G Major, Z. 641 — 63

Corant in G Major, Z. 644 — 64

Minuet in G Major, Z. 651 — 66

Voluntary in G Major, Z. 720 — 66

Song Tune, Z. T694 — 69

March in C Major, Z. 647 — 70

March in C Major, Z. 648 — 71

New Minuet in D Minor, Z. T689 — 72

Minuet in A Minor, Z. 649 — 73

Minuet in A Minor, Z. 650 — 74

A New Scotch Tune, Z. 655 — 75

A New Ground, Z. T682 — 76

Lilliburlero. A New Irish Tune, Z. 646 — 79

Rigadoon, Z. 653 — 80

Sefauchi's Farewell, Z. 656 — 80

Minuet in D Minor, Z. T688 — 82

Almand [Gavotte] in D Major, Z. D219/1 — 83

Borry [Saraband] in D Major, Z. D219/2 — 84

Verse in the Phrygian Mode — 84

The Queen's Dolour. A Farewell, Z. 670 — 86

Minuet in E Minor, Z. D225 — 87

A Ground in D Minor, Z. D222 — 88

PREFACE

DURING the last fifty years several collections of Purcell's Harpsichord Music have appeared. Some of these contain compositions which are now known to have been ascribed to him wrongly, while from time to time various new pieces have come to light. It is believed that the following pages contain all the original compositions that at present can be attributed to him with any degree of certainty. Arrangements (though many are probably from his pen) have been excluded, with the exception of the " New Ground," from " Musick's Handmaid "—a transcription of the air, " Here the Deities approve," from the 1683 St. Cecilia Ode. This has been retained, as the harpsichord version appeared during Purcell's lifetime, though without the name of the composer.

Tempi and marks of expression have been added; but as they are not to be found in the originals, they may be varied according to the taste of the performer. It should be noted that in Purcell's time the *tempo* was supposed to be regulated by the time-signature. But, possibly owing to careless editing, the earliest editions (such as that of the "Choice Collection of Lessons," in which Purcell's Suites appeared in 1699) do not with any consistency carry out the rules laid down. It appears, however, certain that the *tempi* of the various dance-movements of the Suites (*e.g.*, the Corants) differed considerably in England from those in use in France. With regard to the Graces, so important a feature in Harpsichord Music, the original signs have been retained. Their meaning will be easily understood by studying the following rules, which were prefixed to the " Choice Collection of Lessons " (1699) and other similar collections:—

RULES FOR GRACES.

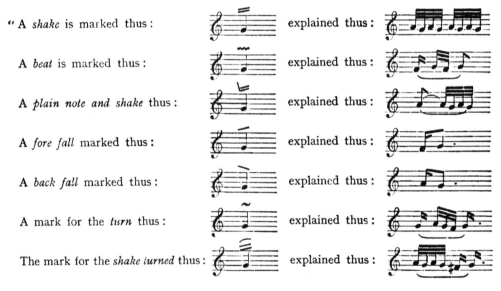

Observe that you always *shake* from the note above, and *beat* from the note or half-note below, according to the key you play in " [*i.e.*, graces are diatonic and shakes generally begin with the upper accessory]; "and for the *plain note and shake*" [*i.e.*, appoggiatura and shake], "if it be a note without a point " [*i.e.*, undotted], "you are to hold half the quantity of it plain, and that upon the note above tha which is marked and shake the other half, but if it be a note with a point to it" [*i.e.*, a dotted note], "you are to hold all the note plain and shake only the point" [*i.e.*, the appoggiatura takes about half the value of the main note; if the main note is dotted, two-thirds].

" A *slur* is marked thus: explained thus:

The mark for the *battery* thus: explained thus:

In Dannreuther's " Musical Ornamentation " (to which the student may be referred who wishes to pursue further the interesting subject of obsolete graces) it is shown that the *battery*, in modern notation, would be written thus:

PUBLISHER'S NOTE

This volume reproduces all the music, in its original order, from the four-volume set *Suites, Lessons and Pieces for the Harpsichord* published by J. & W. Chester. However, the names of many of the pieces have been changed to those given in Franklin B. Zimmerman's *Henry Purcell, 1659–1695: An Analytical Catalogue of His Music*, and Zimmerman's catalogue numbers have been supplied. The equivalents are as follows:

Chester ed.	*Dover ed.*
Suite I	Suite in G Major, Z. 660
Suite II	Suite in G Minor, Z. 661
Suite III	Suite in G Major, Z. 662
Suite IV	Suite in A Minor, Z. 663
Suite V	Suite in C Major, Z. 666
Suite VI	Suite in D Major, Z. 667
Suite VII	Suite in D Minor, Z. 668
Suite VIII	Suite in F Major, Z. 669
Trumpet Tune, called the Cebell	Trumpet Tune, called the Cibell, Z. T678
Air	Trumpet Tune in C Major, Z. T697
A Ground in Gamut	A Ground in Gamut, Z. 645
Air	Almand in C Major, from Suite, Z. 665
Lesson	Saraband with Division, Z. 654
Voluntary	Voluntary in C Major, Z. 717
Verse	A Verse in F Major, Z. 716
Trumpet Tune	Trumpet Tune in D Major
Air	Air in D Minor, Z. T675
Air	Air in D Minor, Z. T676
Ground	Ground in C Minor, Z. T681
Prelude	Prelude in A Minor, Z. 652
Toccata	Toccata in A Major, Z. D229
Hornpipe	Hornpipe in E Minor, Z. T685
Air	Air in G Major, Z. 641
Corant	Corant in G Major, Z. 644
Minuet	Minuet in G Major, Z. 651
Prelude	Voluntary in G Major, Z. 720
Twelve Lessons from 'Musick's Handmaid', Part II:	
I. Song Tune	Song Tune, Z. T694
II.	March in C Major, Z. 647
III. March	March in C Major, Z. 648
IV. New Minuet	New Minuet in D Minor, Z. T689
V. Minuet	Minuet in A Minor, Z. 649
VI. Minuet	Minuet in A Minor, Z. 650
VII. A New Scotch Tune	A New Scotch Tune, Z. 655
VIII. A New Ground	A New Ground, Z. T682
IX. A New Irish Tune. Lilliburlero	Lilliburlero. A New Irish Tune, Z. 646
X. Rigadoon	Rigadoon, Z. 653
XI. Sefauchi's Farewell	Sefauchi's Farewell, Z. 656
XII. Minuet	Minuet in D Minor, Z. T688
Almand	Almand [Gavotte] in D Major, Z. D219/1
Borry	Borry [Saraband] in D Major, Z. D219/2
Prelude	Verse in the Phrygian Mode
The Queen's Dolour. A Farewell	The Queen's Dolour. A Farewell, Z. 670
Minuet	Minuet in E Minor, Z. D225
A Ground	A Ground in D Minor, Z. D222

Suite in G Major

Z. 660

PRELUDE. Andantino. (♩ = 112.)

ALMAND. Andantino. (♩ = 112)

CORANT. Andante. (♩ = 112)

3

MINUET. Andante. (♩=112.)

Suite in G Minor
Z. 661

PRELUDE. Allegretto. (♩=96.)

ALMAND. Andante. (ρ=108.)

CORANT. Maestoso. (♩=88.)

SARABAND. Adagio. (♩ = 72.)

Suite in G Major
Z. 662

12

ALMAND. Maestoso. (♩ = 80.)

14

CORANT. Andante (♩ = 88.)

Suite in A Minor

Z. 663

CORANT. Maestoso. (♩=84.)

SARABAND. Adagio. (♩ = 84.)

Suite in C Major
Z. 666

ALMAND. Andantino. (♩ = 112.)

CORANT. Maestoso. (♩= 84.

SARABAND. Andante. (♩= 84.)

Suite in D Major
Z. 667

PRELUDE. Allegretto. ♩ = 100.

27

HORNPIPE. Allegretto. ♩=76.

Suite in D Minor

Z. 668

ALMAND.
Very slow. ♩ = 60.

30

CORANT. Andante. ♩=84.

HORNPIPE. **Allegretto.** (♩=108.)

Suite in F Major

Z. 669

PRELUDE. Allegretto. (♩=108.)

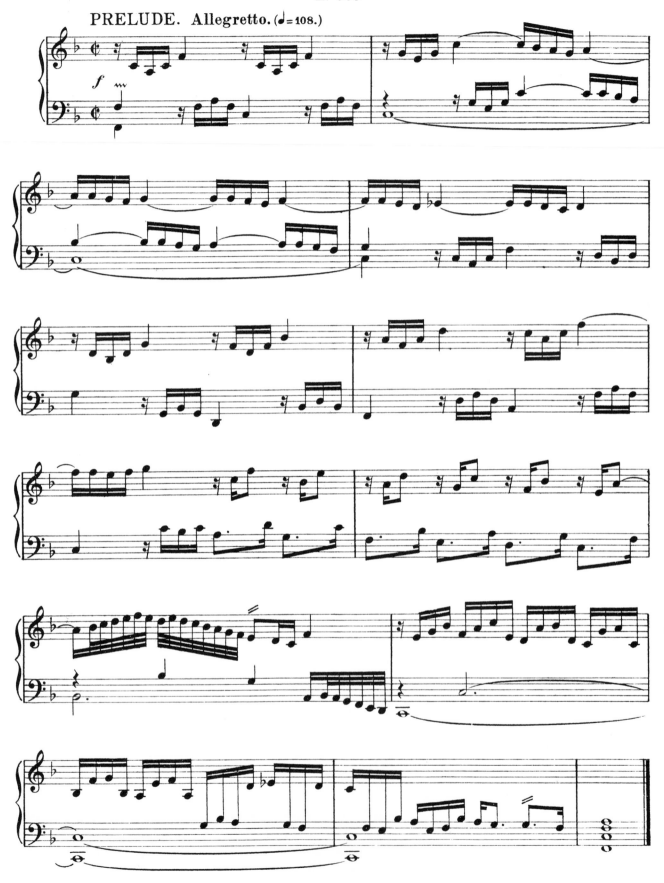

ALMAND. Maestoso. (♩=76.)

CORANT. Andante. ($=76$)

35

MINUET. Allegretto. ($\quad$ = 112)

Trumpet Tune, called the Cibell
Z. T678

38

Trumpet Tune in C Major

(from *Dioclesian*)

Z. T697

A Ground in Gamut

Z. 645

Almand in C Major

from Suite, Z. 665

Saraband with Division

Z. 654

Voluntary in C Major

(for organ)

Z. 717

A Verse in F Major

(for organ)

Z. 716

Trumpet Tune in D Major

(actually by Jeremiah Clarke)

Air in D Minor

(originally intended for *The Indian Queen*)

Z. T675

Air in D Minor

(from *The Double Dealer*)

Z. T676

48

Ground in C Minor

("With Him He Brings the Partner," from
Ye Tuneful Muses)

Z. T681

49

Prelude in A Minor
Z. 652

Toccata in A Major

(probably not by Purcell)

Z. D229

Allegro (tempo primo.)

Hornpipe in E Minor

(from *The Old Bachelor*)

Z. T685

Air in G Major

Z. 641

Corant in G Major
Z. 644

66

Minuet in G Major

Z. 651

Voluntary in G Major

(for organ)

Z. 720

68

Song Tune

("Ah! How Pleasant 'tis to Love")

Z. T694

March in C Major
Z. 647

March in C Major

Z. 648

New Minuet in D Minor

("Who Can Resist Such Mighty Charms,"
from *Timon of Athens*)

Z. T689

Minuet in A Minor

Z. 649

Minuet in A Minor
Z. 650

A New Scotch Tune

Z. 655

A New Ground in E Minor

("Here the Deities Approve," from
Welcome to All the Pleasures)

Z. T682

Lilliburlero. A New Irish Tune
Z. 646

Rigadoon
Z. 653

Sefauchi's Farewell
Z. 656

Minuet in D Minor

(from *Raise, Raise the Voice*)

Z. T688

Almand [Gavotte] in D Major
(probably not by Purcell)
Z. D219/1

Borry [Saraband] in D Major

(probably not by Purcell)

Z. D219/2

Verse in the Phrygian Mode

(for organ; actually by Nicolas-Antoine Lebègue)

The Queen's Dolour. A Farewell

Z. 670

Minuet in E Minor
(probably not by Purcell)
Z. D225

A Ground in D Minor

(probably not by Purcell)

Z. D222